presents

sabina!

by Chris Dolan

Borderline Theatre Company
– is funded by
The Scottish Arts Council,
South Ayshire Council
East Ayrshire Council
– received sponsorship from

digital
Digital Equipment Scotland Ltd.

Registered Charity number: SC000564

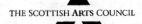

Borderline Theatre Company

Borderline Theatre Company was born out of a great passion and enthusiasm for high quality, accessible theatre held by a group of people in Ayrshire in the early seventies.

In its first year the Company toured ten productions across Ayrshire playing to audiences in venues ranging from converted Nissen huts to Victorian town halls. Within two years Borderline were selling-out at London's Royal Court with Billy Connolly's *An Me Wi' A Bad Leg Tae*, a hilarious tale about family life in a Glasgow tenement. Audiences clearly shared the enthusiasm for Borderline's new exciting style of theatre.

With Borderline's reputation for providing a 'good night out' established, its work throughout the seventies went from strength to strength, enabling the company to work with the best in Scottish talent. 1977 saw the commission of Billy Connolly's second play *When Hair was Long, And Time Was Short*, which won the company its first Edinburgh Fringe First. John Byrne became Writer-in-Residence in 1978, continuing an extremely fruitful relationship with the company that in future years led to such successful productions as *Cara Coco* and *Dick Whittington* starring Robbie Coltrane as the coolest cat you would ever hope to see.

By 1979 the company had gained a new Artistic Director, Morag Fullarton and a reputation as a company that would present bold and entertaining productions. None more so than *Guys and Dolls*, performed by a cast of eight – who all played their part as the Hotbox dancers!

Morag Fullarton is recognised as the person responsible for introducing Scotland to Dario Fo through her string of Fo successes – *Can't Pay, Won't Pay*, *Female Parts*, *Trumpets and Raspberries* and Robbie Coltrane's one-man tour de force in *Mistero Buffo*, which was subsequently screened on BBC2.

What made these productions even more special for the company was Fo's visit to see *Trumpets and Raspberries* which he proclaimed 'the best production I have seen outside Italy'. Borderline were of course delighted when Dario Fo won the 1997 Nobel Prize for Literature.

Morag wrote and directed many of the company's extremely successful productions including *Play it Again Tam*, which won Borderline's second Fringe First and *Glasvegas* – with its unforgettable strapline, 'Some are born great, some are made great and some are still chucking spears at the buses.'

By the mid-eighties the company had outgrown its initial home of the Harbour Arts Centre in Irvine and moved to a disused church in central Ayr. This provided the company with the necessary storage, office and rehearsal space.

In the early nineties John Murtagh as Artistic Director led the company to such successful productions as *Waiting for Tommy*, a tragi-comic one-man show about Tommy Cooper.

1993 saw Borderline pick up two awards. The first was a Fringe First for A. L. Kennedy's *The Audition* and the second was the *Evening News* Capital Award for *The Guid Sodjer Schweik*, adapted from Jaroslav Hasek's novel.

In 1994 Borderline received another accolade, but this time in the form of an endorsement from one of Hollywood's legends being in the audience. Jack Lemmon attended one of the performances of Neil Simon's classic *The Odd Couple* at the Assembly Rooms. This production starring Craig Ferguson and Gerard Kelly was the smash hit of Scottish theatre that year, with just under 30,000 people seeing the show in 52 performances.

Borderline has always championed theatre for young people, who are not only an audience in their own right but also tomorrow's audiences, writers, actors. directors, designers and technicians. The company's commitment to this important aspect of the art form is reflected in the calibre of playwrights whose work Borderline have toured; Stuart Paterson, Liz Lochhead, Tom McGrath, Harry Enfield, Bryan Elsley and Gerry Mulgrew.

The Misanthrope, 1997

It seemed only natural then that for Borderline the whole issue of access to the arts should develop into a practical manifestation. In addition to his main house directing work, John Murtagh took on the task of developing the company's outreach programme to work in communities through workshops, youth theatres and issue-based productions to make drama as accessible as possible to as many people as possible. This strand of the company's work has gone from strength to strength, aiming to create closer links with the main house touring work and now works with clients as diverse as special needs groups, nursery/primary/secondary pupils, youth groups, in fact anyone who would like to be involved in drama. This has all gone to make Borderline unique in that they are the only Scottish touring theatre company that has an extensive outreach and education programme throughout the year.

1997 brought Borderline their current Artistic Director, Leslie Finlay. His production of Molière's *The Misanthrope* in a new version by Martin Crimp was hailed by critics as 'a cracker of a production' and was 'a highlight of the year'. The company's 1997 school's production was Lin Coghlan's *Broken Angel* which dealt with the sensitive issue of alcohol abuse. The show was so successful that it had to be re-toured because of the demand from schools.

In the coming years Borderline is committed to presenting a vibrant touring programme that will be a combination of new writing that will significantly contribute to the repertoire of Scottish plays and classic texts presented in a fresh way. The company's investment in the future has already started with partnerships with writers of the calibre of Chris Dolan and Anita Sullivan which will produce work of the highest quality. This investment is vital as Borderline aims to continue to meet the hunger for exciting and challenging touring theatre demanded by audiences.

Borderline stands today as one of the premier Scottish touring theatre companies which has consistently presented quality theatre and worked with the best actors, writers, designers etc. In fact a roll call of past Borderline employees reads like a veritable 'who's who' of Scottish theatre. Over the years the company has toured all over Scotland, including the Islands, appeared at the Festival Fringe 18 times and developed a solid audience support. Borderline's status as one of the leading touring company's was recently confirmed by the Scottish Arts Council when they agreed to continue funding the company's work into the new Millennium.

From the vision of a group of theatre lovers in the seventies, Borderline is still growing in terms of artistic vision and audience. If one statement were required to characterise the Company and its work it would be that it opens the door to theatre, sharing its pleasures and enjoyment with its audience. Borderline's passion to present accessible quality theatre remains undiminished.

The Angels' Share

by Chris Dolan

WORLD PREMIERE
directed by Leslie Finlay

A story of love gone wrong and conflict within a tight-knit island community between father and daughter, the past and the present and traditional values and new economics

When Edward McLean leaves London to turn around the family business he is confident that he will be both the company and the island's salvation. Determined to make his mark at any cost and distracted by his love for his cousin Mairead, McLean soon finds himself the centre of a seething web of sexual jealousy, mistrust and resentment.

Empowered by the changes he has already made, Mairead and her lover Paraig challenge the remaining old order, forcing McLean to take drastic action to make his mission a success and to win Mairead.

As he plunges the island's livelihood into chaos, ultimately destroying Mairead's happiness, McLean finds himself cast out and facing his nemesis.

The Angels' Share will premiere at the 1998 Edinburgh Festival Fringe

TOURING AUGUST/SEPTEMBER/OCTOBER 1998

For further information please contact

Borderline Theatre Company
North Harbour Street
Ayr KA8 8AA

Tel: 01292 281010   Fax: 01292 263825

sabina!

by Chris Dolan

Cast

Sandra	Lorraine McGowan
Tereza	Jane Stabler
Matthew	Vincent Friell

Director	Leslie Finlay
Designer	Elaine Robertson
Music	Ross Campbell
Lighting Designer	Bevis Evans-Teush
Stage Manager	Keith Bruce
Deputy Stage Manager	Viktoria Begg
Assistant Stage Manager	Paul Ancell

Setting

Glasgow in the days leading up to the Velvet Revolution in Czechoslovakia in 1989

Persons are not allowed to sit or stand in any of the aisles. The Management reserves the right to refuse admission and to make any alteration in the cast which may be rendered necessary by illness or other unavoidable causes. Patrons are reminded that smoking is not permitted in the auditorium. No photographs, to be taken or video or sound recordings to be made

Chris Dolan

Chris Dolan has been writing full-time for the screen, stage and page since 1991. *Sabina!* is his first full-length play, which won a Fringe First in 1996 and subsequently toured Northern Spain and was the centrepiece of the Milan International Arts Festival in 1997.

He won the 1995 McCallan/Scotland on Sunday Short Story Prize for *Sleet and Snow*, which was taken from his collection of short stories called *Poor Angels*, which itself was shortlisted for the Saltire prize. Three stories from this collection were also the basis of three short plays that were premiered at the Citizens Theatre in 1997. In 1993 he won the Scottish Screenwriters Award and adapted Bill Douglas's last screenplay, *Ring of Truth*, for the BBC.

Chris is currently working on a new play commission, *The Angels' Share*, for Borderline that will be premiered at the 1998 Edinburgh Festival, and a new novel called *Ascension Day*. He also lectures in writing and literature, and is presently Writer in Residence in Easterhouse, Glasgow.

Lorraine McGowan

Graduated in Drama and English from Glasgow University. Theatre credits include: *The Lion in Winter* (Perth Rep.), *Sabina!* and *Romeo and Juliet* (New Stage Theatre), *Puppy Dogs' Tales, The Theory and Practice of Belly Dancing, Wedding Bells and Green Grasses* (Chimera Theatre Company), *Lyon Rampant* (Eyas Theatre Company), *Crimes of the Heart* (Bare Bones Theatre Company), *Cafe Ole* and *Christmas Cracker* (Random Harvest Theatre Company) *Ms Shiah* (Roughcast Theatre Company).

Television and film includes: *Nitrate Won't Wait* (STV/Centenary Reels), *Number Thirteen* (Ro.Ro. Productions), *Althetico Partick* and *F.O.T* (BBC). Lorraine is also a founder member, co-writer and performer with comedy cabaret trio *Pretty Vacant*.

Jane Stabler

Trained at Royal Scottish Academy of Music and Drama, graduating in 1995. Theatre work includes Viola in *Twelfth Night* and Capulet in *Romeo and Juliet* (Theatre Babel), Hero in *Much Ado about Nothing* (Original Shakespeare Company), Tereza in *Sabina!* (New Stage Theatre); Felice in *Kafka Dances* (HighDoh), Mary Gallagher in *The Good Times Will Come* (Dogstar).

Film work includes Alison in *Wanting and Getting* (Ch 4), Maria in *Going Down* (BBC) and Emma in *The Acid House* (Ch 4).

Vincent Friell

Graduated from the Royal Scottish Academy of Music and Drama. Theatre credits include: *The Slab Boys Trilogy, Hard Times, Uncle Vanya, White Bird Passes* (Dundee Rep.), *Tally's Blood* (Traverse), *Men Should Weep, The Lucky Ones* and *The Tempest* (TAG Theatre Co.), *Arsenic and Old Lace* (Citizens Theatre), *Danton's Death* (Communicado Theatre Co), *The Slab Boys Trilogy* (Young Vic).

Film and television includes: *Restless Natives* (EMI), *Trainspotting, Silent Scream* (Antonine Productions), *Blood Red Roses* (Freeway), *Taggart* (STV), *Roughnecks* (First Choice/Ashling Walsh), *End of The Line* (BBC), *Knockback* (BBC), *Parahandy* (BBC), *Rab C. Nesbitt* (BBC), *Country Diary of an Edwardian Lady* (Granada), *Take the High Road* (STV).

Leslie Finlay

Trained at King Alfred's College, Winchester, graduating with BA (Hons) Drama, Theatre and Television. Awarded the Scottish Arts Council Associate Bursary in 1993 attached to TAG Theatre.

He became Artistic Director for Borderline Theatre in January 1997, and has since directed Molière's *The Misanthrope* in a new version by Martin Crimp, two tours of *Broken Angel* by Lin Coghlan, and *Street Scenes* by Anita Sullivan in partnership with South Ayrshire Council. His work with TAG Theatre included Liz Lochhead's *The Magic Island* and the world premiere of *The Keeper of the Keys* by Vivien Adam. He was also Assistant Director on TAG's *As You Like It*.

Finlay founded and was Artistic Director of New Stage Theatre from 1990 to 1997, and in 1996 their production of *Sabina!* won a Fringe First Award at the Edinburgh Festival. *Sabina!* then went onto represent Scotland at the Milan International Arts Festival. Other works with New Stage Theatre include *Romeo and Juliet,* which toured Scotland and transferred to Waterman's Theatre, London; *Don Juan Comes Back From the War; Baglady; The Member of the Wedding; The Human Voice* and *Le Bel Indifferent*.

Finlay has also worked as a free-lance director with numerous theatre companies in Scotland and London.

Elaine Robertson

Graduate of Slade School of Fine Art. Design work for Borderline Theatre includes; *Street Scenes, Broken Angel* (both tours). Design work for Citizens Theatre includes *Acting Up* and, as resident design assistant, *Don Carlos, Hamlet, Shadow of a Gunman, Long Day's Journey into Night* and *The Country Wife*. Other design work: *La Finta Giardiniera* (Opera Zuid, Maastricht), *Two Fiddlers* (McRobert Arts Centre), *Sabina!* (New Stage Theatre Company), *No Expense Spared* (Wildcat Stage Productions) and *The Robbers* (Gate Theatre, London). Elaine was also a finalist in the 1995 Winbury Prize for Stage Design.

Ross Campbell

Studied at the Royal College of Music, London with Edwin Roxburgh, winning the Cobbett Prize for composition.

His works have been performed by the Scottish Chamber Orchestra, Paragon Ensemble and the Athelas Sinfonietta of Copenhagen. His score for the short film *Poor Angels*, performed by the BT Scottish Ensemble, was a BAFTA nominee.

Ross Campbell has also been heavily involved in pop music, working as a writer, producer and dance re-mixer from Los Angeles to Glasgow. He has recently worked with the Nightcrawlers and has a forthcoming 'drum and bass' album under the guise of *Scarlet Lake*. He is in constant demand as a composer for film, television and theatre, and lecturers at both the Royal Scottish Academy of Music and Drama and North Glasgow College.

Bevis Evans-Teush

Lighting design for Borderline Theatre includes *The Misanthrope*. Other lighting design work: *Goldielocks* (Scottish Chamber Orchestra), *Knives in Hens* (Traverse Theatre and Bush Theatre), *Sabina!* (New Stage Theatre). Bevis also works in corporate production live events combining video, lighting and graphic techniques. Recent work in this area includes *Greysteel* (National Lottery), *Aladdin* (King's Theatre, Glasgow) and *Fireworks* (Glasgow City Council).

Thanks to

Phil Dagleish and Chris Hendry,
    Digital Equipment Scotland Ltd.
Chris Giles, Giles Insurance Brokers
Andy Howitt
Laurence McNicholas
Sadie and Bill Finlay
Waterstones, Glasgow

Committed to developing arts in the community

South Ayrshire Council is committed to developing arts in the community. The council supports several initiatives by organisations such as Ayr Festival, South Ayrshire Music Festival, Girvan Folk Festival and Girvan Jazz Festival which enhance the life of the community.

Working in partnership to develop Scotland's new School of Music and Recording Technology

In partnership with Enterprise Ayrshire, the University of Paisley and Ayr College, South Ayrshire Council is currently working with project champion Benny Gallagher to develop Scotland's new School of Music and Recording Technology at Dam Park, Ayr.

For further information contact Geoff Coleman, Corporate Support Unit, South Ayrshire Council, County Buildings, Wellington Square, Ayr KA7 1DR.
Tel: 01292 612650

Playwright's Notes

The Mystery of Sabina Vasiliev is based on a story a colleague once told me. There was a man who went around the west end of Glasgow calling himself Jan Danocek. Told everyone, including his fiancée, he was an exiled Czech dissident. In reality, according to my colleague, Jan wasn't Czech at all, but lived with his mother in the south side of the city, and his name was actually Jim Smith or somesuch. I left that job not long after hearing this and never found out what happened to Jim/Jan or his future wife.

I set about writing a story, then a play, based on the idea, mentioned it to friends, and came across tale after tale of people who had lived or acted out a similar kind of lie. I heard of a woman on Skye who swears blind she's French even though everyone knows her utterly Scots parents. Heard endless stories of girls going to night-clubs and making up new identities for themselves. (After the first night of an early version of *Sabina!* I saw some guys who had been in the audience chatting up girls in a nearby bar, pretending they were Australian actors.) Some of these real-life Walter Mittys were simply mischievous, some eccentric, some seriously troubled, lots no doubt made up the products of people's fantasies and exaggerations.

This was 1989, just as the East European regimes were crumbling – a difficult, soul-searching moment for anyone who hopes we can progress beyond brutal capitalism. The following year, coincidentally, I went to Prague and Bratislava to a make a programme about European young people and met a young woman who worked on a samizdat paper and whose whole life had been dedicated to creating in her country a system I had despaired of in my own. Veronika was genuinely heroic, deeply politicised, rebellious – an impressive person who I'm sure would have been on our side in this country, yet who believed ardently in everything that I found limiting and empty.

In my play Jim/Jan became Sandra/Sabina and – as I was reading a lot of Klima and Capek and Kundera at the time – I named the 'real' Czechs in the play Tereza and Tomas. (Later I took to calling my play *The Unbearable Scottishness of Being*.) It struck me that that little second-hand story furnished endless opportunities for exploring themes of personal, sexual and political truth. Such a simple act of pretending to be someone you're not is timeless and almost too big. The best I could do was just tell Sandra's story, revel a bit in her comic situation and let the ironies and morals chime for themselves. And, as I wrote, the less my play became about Czechoslovakia and the East and it dawned on me that I was actually writing about Glasgow.

Leslie Finlay had contacted me after reading in *Scotland on Sunday*, when I won the McCallan Short Story competition, that I also wanted to write plays. An early version of *Sabina!* had already had a couple of nights's airing by Ronnie McCann for Curam Theatre. The short story version came out not long after in *Poor Angels and Other Stories*. After talking to Leslie I worked on it again. Leslie cast it perfectly and a couple of months later we were in Edinburgh. Fleshed out and intelligently performed and presented, *Sabina!* caught on, won us a Fringe First – and, most importantly sold out.

I was surprised that a Festival audience had taken so much to a play that seemed to me totally Glaswegian. Sandra's mentality, the sense of being hidden away behind the endless grey clouds, the unchangeableness of life, the disempowerment of working people far from the seat of power, were all notions that I thought wouldn't have much resonance beyond my city. But as well as Edinburgh's international audience, we've since been to Milan (a place Sandra names in the play as being where everything must be better – an idea that had the Milanese holding their sides and shaking their heads); and the play's been translated into Spanish and toured in Spain. Seems a lot of us – even since the political changes in this country last year – feel sidelined, caged in, Glaswegian to a degree. Then again, we can all of us least dream of change, real change – and revel in the prospect of someone else getting into moral and personal fankles, trying to make a wee dream come true. I wish Jan Danocek well. Hope his fiancée found out about Jim Smith, and didn't chuck him as a result.

Chris Dolan

Tour Schedule

12-14 February	Cumbernauld Theatre
17-21 February	Dundee Repertory Theatre
23-24 February	Lemon Tree, Aberdeen
25 February	Stewart's Hall, Huntly
26 February	Elgin Town Hall
27 February	Fraserburgh Arts Centre
28 February	Banchory Town Hall
3-21 March	The Pleasance, London
24 March	Eden Court, Inverness
25 March	Adam Smith Theatre, Kirkcaldy
26 March	Lochside Theatre, Castle Douglas
27 March	Harbour Arts Centre, Irvine
31 March	McRobert Arts Centre, Stirling
1 April	Gaiety Theatre, Ayr
2 April	Palace Theatre, Kilmarnock
3 April	Barrfields Pavilion, Largs

Can You Make a Contribution?

A man has no ears for that which experience has given him no access.   Friedrich Nietzsche

Borderline's passion for theatre is based on the special experience that only theatre can give the audience and the belief that access to that experience can make a real difference to people's lives. A dictionary definition of access – 'a right of way' – is central to our mission is to provide 'a right of way' through our main stage, touring, outreach and educational work. With your help more people could be given that 'right of way'.

'**Borderline** is blessed with a wonderful sense of humour and the talent to exploit it . . . qualities which make it one of the most attractive theatre companies in Scotland, whose contribution is vital to theatre accessibility.'

Allen Wright, Former Arts Editor, *The Scotsman*

THEY MADE A CONTRIBUTION

This national tour of *Sabina!* was sponsored by Digital Equipment Scotland Ltd. and the Ayrshire performances were sponsored by Giles Insurance Brokers. We gratefully acknowledge their support.

YOU CAN MAKE A DIFFERENCE

We are seeking sponsors for Borderline's touring theatre productions and our outreach and education programme development work. We can design sponsorship packages for your organisation which will be founded in a mutually beneficial partnership approach.

With your help we can continue to make a contribution

Please contact: Eddie Jackson,
Chief Executive,
Borderline Theatre Company,
North Harbour Street,
Ayr KA8 8AA

Tel: 01292 281010
Fax: 01292 263825

Staff

Artistic Director	**Leslie Finlay**
Chief Executive	**Eddie Jackson**
Administrator	**Sally Stewart**
Secretary/Bookkeeper	**Joyce Miller**
Projects Co-ordinator	**Helen Coughtrie**
Workshop Director	**Louise Brown**
Marketing Consultant	**Morag Ballantyne**

Board Members

James Thomson (*Chairman*)
Jan Cunningham
Phil Dagleish
Cllr. Liz Foulkes
Tom Holden
David Johnson (*Vice Chair*)
Elizabeth Moriarty
Peter Occleston
William Porterfield
Sandra Scott
Fiona Scott-Brown
Ian Smillie
Christine Stanley
Cllr. Ian Welsh
Forbes Watson
Ian Woodburn

Chris Dolan
The Mystery of Sabina Vasiliev

faber and faber
LONDON · BOSTON

First published in 1998
by Faber and Faber Limited
3 Queen Square London WC1N 3AU

Typeset by Country Setting, Woodchurch, Kent TN26 3TB
Printed in England by Intype London Ltd

All rights reserved

© Chris Dolan, 1998

Chris Dolan is hereby identified as author
of this work in accordance with Section 77 of the
Copyright, Designs and Patents Act 1988

All rights whatsoever in this work are strictly reserved.
Applications for permission for any use whatsoever,
including performance rights, must be made in advance,
prior to any such proposed use, to Peters, Fraser and Dunlop,
503–4 The Chambers, Chelsea Harbour, London SW10 0XF.
No performance may be given unless a licence has first
been obtained

*This book is sold subject to the condition that it shall not, by
way of trade or otherwise, be lent, resold, hired out or otherwise
circulated without the publisher's prior consent in any form of
binding or cover other than that in which it is published and
without a similar condition including this condition being
imposed on the subsequent purchaser*

A CIP record for this book
is available from the British Library

ISBN 0–571–19590–3

2 4 6 8 10 9 7 5 3 1

Characters

Sandra
Tereza
Matthew

*For Moira Leven
Emma and Daniel*

The Mystery of Sabina Vasiliev

Stage dark. Rain dripping somewhere from a leaky roof. The sound of keys as someone opens the door. The door opens, pouring a dim light from the back across the stage. The silhouette of a woman holding a carrier bag.

Sandra Tereza?

Sandra steps inside. Clicks the light switch – it doesn't come on. She stands on a chair and takes out the light bulb hanging overhead. She takes another bulb out of her pocket and screws it in. It flashes on as she does so.

Ay ya hoor, ye.

We can see the room clearly now: the front room of a basic flat. Radio, cardboard boxes full of books, etc. Sandra wanders around, looking at everything. Takes a book out of a box.

(*Reads title.*) Zahradní Slavnost.

Puts book back. Goes to her carrier bag. Takes a new dress out of the bag, holds it up to inspect it. Pulls off her jacket and starts to unbutton her shirt. Then she shivers, shrugs; pulls the dress on over her shirt and jeans. Spins round.

Czechoslovakia. Ceskoslovensko.

Behind her, Tereza appears at the door in a long coat and fur hat. She watches amazed as Sandra, not noticing her, dances around with her new dress, chanting.

Ceskoslovensko.

On a spin she catches sight of Tereza.

Christ on a bike! How did you get there?

Tereza What are you doing?

Tereza has a foreign accent.

Sandra Fixing a light bulb. What does it look like?

Tereza What on earth are you wearing?

Tereza takes off her shoes at the door.

Sandra I've noticed that. You never wear shoes in the house. Why's that? Do they pinch you?

Tereza No.

Sandra Mine do. They're pure murder. See if you're ever looking for me, just follow the trail of blood. I take a size smaller than I should.

Tereza Why?

Sandra I take everything a size smaller. That way you stop yourself from getting fat.

Tereza That is very lack-brained.

Sandra Lack-brained?

Tereza Blunt-witted.

Sandra Who in the name of the wee society man taught you English? Willy Shakespeare?

Tereza Yes, used his texts, and other great tomes in our class.

Sandra Well, it's neither blunt-brained or lack-witted. I like tight clothes. It's like the feeling you used to get when you were wee and your mother tucked you up tight in bed. What's your excuse?

Tereza For what?

Sandra Wearing shoes that are too wee for you.

Tereza I don't.

Sandra Then how come you never wear any in the house?

Tereza Habit, I suppose. Prague is very dirty. If you don't take your shoes off, you drag dust everywhere.

Sandra Can't be as dirty as here.

Tereza begins to unpack books from the boxes.

Tereza Dirtier.

Sandra Can't be.

Tereza It is. Believe me.

Sandra Never.

Tereza It *is,* Sandra. Please. I live there.

Sandra Well if this place is so bloody spotless, why do you bother taking off your shoes?

Tereza I told you – a habit of a lifetime. Now I'm more comfortable without them.

Sandra So. I was right – they *are* too small for you.

Tereza Good God!

Sound of roof leaking in the silence.

That bloody roof. I've been round at the factors twice now.

Sandra Doesn't bother me.

Tereza Nothing bothers you. Why are you here anyway? I thought you were out tonight.

Sandra I cancelled. You're giving me my Czech language lesson tonight.

Tereza Not tonight.

Sandra You changed my night, remember? You said that whatsisname was coming tomorrow, and I should come tonight. Not remember?

Tereza It was the other way round. I changed him to tonight so you could have your lesson as usual. That's what we agreed.

Sandra That can't be right. That would mean that you organised him in the first place for tomorrow which you knew was my night. You would just have organised him for tonight, which you didn't, so I changed my lesson from tomorrow to tonight. See?

Tereza No.

Sandra I think you just don't want me to meet him.

Tereza Of course I want you to meet him. He'll need to see his new tenant.

Tereza Unless of course you *wanted* to meet him tonight. Is that why you're dressed up?

Sandra *I* don't want to meet him. You're the one who deals with him. Why would I want to meet the owner of a dump like this?

Tereza Because you like him. You told me you like him.

Sandra I said I *knew* him. The verb 'to know'. Quite distinct from the verb to like. Anyway that was years ago. Before he went into the property business.

Tereza He's *not* in the property business. He let me have this place as a favour.

Sandra Now why is it I'm suspicious of a man who lets you stay in his flat for a favour?

Tereza slumps down on a chair, tired.

Tereza It's hardly worth it. He's had me talking to nearly every class in his school! As well as teaching him Czech. *And* keeping an eye on you.

Sandra On me? First I've heard of that!

Tereza Well not you, specifically. Matthew thinks Scottish people are irresponsible tenants.

Sandra That a fact? Big Jessie T-biscuit.

Tereza Excuse me? The last two here had parties every night. He wants me to make sure it doesn't happen again.

Sandra So how come you picked me?

Tereza You seemed like a quiet girl.

Sandra Yeh. Thanks. Nice wee, quiet Sandra. That's me.

Silence for a moment. Tereza gets up and starts unpacking again.

I should've strutted my stuff more at school. Maybe I'd've got noticed. Not by *him*, in particular, you understand. Wouldn't've made any difference if I had.

Tereza Why?

Sandra And this isn't getting dressed up, by the way. Just dressed. You don't want me to meet him naked do you?

Tereza I wouldn't put it past you. Just, you don't normally wear dresses.

Sandra If I was going to wear this tonight, I'd have bought shoes. With trainers on, I'd only be dressed from the dress up. It just so happens that I thought I might go out tonight. After my lesson – which *was* arranged for tonight. At least my body fancied a night out, but my legs wanted to stay in, so they didn't buy anything. Which means all of me'll probably have to stay in. If the legs don't go, I've no means of transport.

Tereza What?

Sandra takes off the dress.

Sandra I'm saying, it's not me that's boring. Just my legs.

Sandra watches Tereza unpacking. She lifts a gun, on a plinth, out of the box, puts it on the bookshelf.

What's *that* for!

Tereza A souvenir.

Sandra Christ. Some place Czechoslovakia. Here we tend to go for plates with Edinburgh Castle on them. Mind you, *they* can be handy in square-go. My old man nearly decapitated me once with a 'Welcome to Bonnie Loch Lomond' cheese dish.

Tereza It was my father's.

Sandra picks it up.

Sandra Is it loaded?

Tereza shrugs. Goes on unpacking. Sandra puts gun down. After a moment:

Tereza So you're not venturing out tonight?

Sandra Me, venture? Why? Do you want me to?

Tereza I didn't say that.

Sandra If whatsisname's coming, maybe I'd better.

Tereza Do what you like.

Sandra Anyway, it's you he fancies. Obviously.

Tereza Fancies?

Sandra You know, likes you, wants you, has the hots for you, wants to –

Tereza – Be my lover?

Sandra Whoa! Steady on. You're not back in Prague yet. You don't get lovers in this country. It's undemocratic. Anyway, you've already got a lover. Thingamyjig.

Tereza Thingamay? Tomás? Right now Tomás and I are both far too –

Sandra I know. Married to the Revolution and all that. So you're not interested in Matthew?

Tereza Of course not! He's coming round for his lesson – which I *did* arrange for tonight. What makes you think he's interested in me?

Sandra You're Czech, aren't you?

Tereza What's that got to do with it?

Sandra Everyone knows that all Czech women are intelligent and sophisticated and go like bunnies.

Tereza Go like what?

Sandra Make good 'lovers', to use the Czech word.

Tereza Who says?

Sandra It's common knowledge. All Czech women have these great big difficult books which they put under their backs so they can do it in weird positions with all the men. And the guys are all university professors except that they work as window cleaners. Naturally, they read them first. The books. Czech women do. And then they lend them to the men afterwards. In the West it's more acceptable just to have a smoke.

Tereza Amazing. I never knew any of that.

Sandra Look at you – you've been in this flat for over a fortnight, and you're *still* unpacking books. Now that can't be natural. You bring two dresses and a spare pair of knickers from Czechoslovakia, and half the bleedin' Prague library.

Tereza I got the books here. To take home.

Sandra See? There's no way Matthew could resist a Czech woman. Here you are, a dissident and everything. Used to work on a samizdat paper, escaped the country –

Tereza Don't make fun of things like that.

Sandra I'm not making fun. You've lived a very exciting life.

Tereza You and your romantic ideas about revolutions. You want to know what it's really like? It's about waiting. They try to steal your soul and there's only one way to fight them. Wait for your chance to strike. And while you wait, grow harder, colder – keeping them in your sights, watching them down the barrel of a gun.

This is how my people survive.

And at last, when the vital moment arrives to strike, you must make yourself like them. Efficient, resolute. And you strike in cold blood and without pity.

Sandra Wow. That's exciting enough. For such a young thing. How many people do you know that've escaped their country at your age?

Tereza Plenty. Since the Hungarians opened the border to Germany, hundreds probably, squeezing their way through the Berlin Wall.

Sandra I know! Did you see the party they were having on the telly last night? Lucky bastards.

Tereza It's our turn next.

Sandra You haven't got a wall.

Tereza They don't need bricks to build a wall.

Sandra See what I mean? How could it fail!

Tereza Easily! It's touch and go in my country right now.

Sandra I mean Matthew. (*Czech accent*) 'They don't need bricks to build a wall'! How could he fail to fall for someone like you? You've got a revolution to fight. He must be wonderful.

Tereza Matthew? He's alright I –

Sandra No, no. Tomás.

Tereza What makes you think that?

Sandra His name is Tomás. And he comes from Prague. What more do you want?

Tereza Come on. Let's see if we can complete this lesson before Matthew arrives. Did you manage the exercise I gave you?

Sandra takes a jotter out of her carrier bag; hands it to Tereza.

Sandra Dead easy. I did the next section on the future conditional as well.

Tereza goes through the exercise. Sandra looks around the room, waiting. Tereza looks up, surprised.

Tereza My stars! Ten out of ten, both times. You have a real gift, Sandra.

Sandra I told you. Started French at Uni. Until I got bored rigid.

Tereza It really aggrieves me, that. You people all getting 'bored'. If you'd lived in my country, you'd soon appreciate what you have.

Sandra You're joking. Place is a midden.

Sandra goes over to the window and looks out.

Tereza I like it here.

Sandra That's just 'cause you're Czech. Even boring places are interesting first time around. Won't last long, don't you worry.

Pause, as Sandra stares out into the rain.

Soon you'll be like the rest of us.

Pause.

Sometimes, I get the feeling that if I stood in the same place for too long, I'd fade right into the stone. Did you ever get that feeling? Like you'd become fixed, earthed in one spot forever.

Tereza I know the feeling. But not here.

Sandra Well, don't hang around girl or you soon will. If I were you I'd high-tail it back to Prague just as soon as you've had your revolution. Otherwise you'll be sucked up into the Bank of Scotland's portico before you can say a friend for life.

Tereza Sometimes I wonder why I ever bothered to learn English. Do you want this lesson or not?

Sandra shrugs.

Sandra Whatsisface – loverboy – will be here any minute.

Pause.

How come you hardly ever mention this Tom chap?

Tereza Who? Oh Tomás again. I can't keep up with you tonight.

Sandra Where's he now? Back in Prague?

Tereza Yes. Sometimes I get to hear about him, when I get my instructions from Prague.

Sandra Instructions? From Prague! I wish someone would give me instructions from Prague! What kind of instructions?

Tereza Not instructions exactly. News. What I should say when I speak to people here.

Sandra Now if I were the kind of girl that got instructions from Prague, the likes of Matthew might even fancy me –

Tereza Oh, not again. Matthew does not fancify *me*.

Sandra Oh, he fancifies you alright. He'll think you're the kind of girl that'll make love on the tops of buses on your way to secret rendezvous . . . the Mata Hari of Maryhill.

Tereza (*laughs*) You only went to school with him. So how can you tell he wants to make love to me?

Sandra It was a comprehensive school.

Tereza You expect me to believe he would like any woman simply because she is Czech?

Sandra Or even Slovakian. Russian. Who knows – maybe he'd even stoop to a Romanian.

Tereza Pish and tush!

Sandra Pish and what?

Tereza Rot. Balderdash.

Sandra Well maybe it's pish and maybe it's not, but I bet I'm right. How much do you want to bet?

Tereza I don't hold with gambling. And anyway, there's no way of proving it.

Sandra There might be.

Sandra stands up, walks around the room thinking.

We'll put it to the test. When he comes here, we'll pretend that I'm Czech, too. What's the bet he'll end up fancifying the both of us.

Tereza Don't be ridiculous.

Sandra I'm not *that* much uglier than you.

Tereza I don't mean that. I mean pretending you're Czech. How could you?

Sandra Easy. We used to do it all the time.

Tereza Who did?

Sandra Me and the girls. We'd go out to a disco and pretend we were a bunch of Australians or Londoners – or Italians, taking a break from the fashion industry.

Tereza And people believed this?

Sandra As long as you don't take it too far. Jenny Goudie once got off with this guy. She told him she'd just been sacked from the Stock Exchange for being a Maoist spy. They caught her at her computer one day chanting under her breath 'Ho ho ho Chi Minh, we will fight and we will win'. So they booted her out.

Tereza But he didn't believe her, did he? This guy?

Sandra As a matter of fact he did. But that *was* pushing it a bit far. The trick is to know when to stop.

Tereza He must have been an imbecile.

Sandra No. He just wanted a bit of excitement. I mean, who would you rather spend the evening with – a fashion queen from Milan or a Tesco's checkout girl?

Tereza To me they're both quite exotic, actually.

Sandra Christ. You've never been in Tesco's. If you think you have food queues now, just wait till the Tesco girls get there.

Tereza Anyway, your plan won't work in this case. You were at school with Matthew, remember?

Sandra Precisely. See how good a test of my theory it'd be? He's actually seen me before, what's the bets he'll still fall for it. *Two* foreign women? Wild horses couldn't stop him.

The doorbell rings.

There he is! Go on. Give it a try. It'll be a laugh. You could do with a laugh.

Tereza No. I deplore dishonesty.

Sandra Dishonesty my arse. Come on. Just for a while. You're probably right – he probably won't buy it. And even if he does, it's just for a few minutes. You can tell him at the end of the lesson.

Tereza What? Leave me to clear up the mess? No thank you. I've enough on my plate just now.

Sandra Oh, go on. I'll tell him after. He won't mind. Hang on – I'll run and change into this dress. We'll give it a bash.

Sandra takes the carrier bag, and heads for a door.

Tereza Did you have this planned?

Sandra sticks her head round the door.

Sandra Of course not! It's a Tomás I'm after. Not another bloody Matthew!

She withdraws into the room. The bell rings again, twice. Tereza makes her way to the door.

Go on. Get a life!

Tereza No. I want no part of it. I haven't time for foolish pranks.

Sandra appears, combing her hair.

Sandra Forget it then. Spoilsport. It was just a bit of fun.

She goes off again.

Tereza opens the door. Matthew is carrying a bunch of flowers.

Matthew Sorry. Have I got the wrong night?

Tereza No, no. Come in.

Matthew These are for you. (*Hands over flowers.*)

Tereza Oh. Thank you.

Matthew I was worried you were out.

Tereza Me? Of course not. We had a date.

Matthew You look nice tonight.

Tereza Thank you.

Pause.

Tereza Sit down. Shall we begin? The lesson, I mean.

Matthew Yeah, sure. (*He looks around the room.*) Are *all* these books yours?

Tereza Yes.

He picks out a book. Flicks through it. Takes it over to her.

Matthew This is in Czech. Looks interesting. What's it about?

They bend together over the book. Sandra enters, her new dress on, and bare-footed.

Tereza Miroslav Holub.

They see Sandra.

Matthew Hullo. (*to Tereza*) You've found a new flatmate?

Tereza Yes. Matthew, this is San –

Sandra Sabina! Sabina Vasiliev. Very pleased to make your acquaintance.

She puts on an accent. Goes to him; they shake hands.

Tereza has told me very much about you. You're a very humane landowner.

Matthew Me? No. I've just got this place. I'm a teacher really.

Sandra looks him up and down slowly

Sandra Tereza says a very good one. I can see what she means.

Matthew But Tereza's never really seen me teach.

Sandra She's a very good judge of character, aren't you Tereza?

Tereza Clearly not.

Matthew Are you from Prague, too?

Sandra I'm from near Prague. A little village. You'll never have heard of it. Do come in.

Sandra leads Matthew to the centre of the room.

Matthew I've seen you before.

Sandra Oh.

Matthew Once. With Tereza. Coming in here. I was passing in the car. I just presumed you were a Scottish friend of hers.

Sandra That's very kind of you. Scottish girls are so much more beautiful than us Czechs, don't you think?

Matthew Oh no. Quite the contrary. Honestly.

Sandra I'm sure you're just saying that.

Sandra sits on a chair, looks victoriously at Tereza.

Matthew How come all you Czechs speak such good English?

Tereza sits on the sofa.

Tereza Well *my* grandfather was English. (*She pats the sofa beside her.*) Sit down, please.

He does. Turns to Sandra .

Sandra So was mine. That is, my grandmother was.

Tereza He went to Prague with the Communist Youth, met my grandmother, and they fell in love.

They both look at Sandra

Sandra What? Oh. The same. But the other way round. But enough about boring old us. *You're* the interesting one, Martin.

Matthew You must be joking.

Sandra Tell us all about your life in this strange, foreign land.

Matthew Not much to tell really . . . My father's not from here, either. Stirling, actually. Not that Stirling's . . .

Sandra Married? Single? A bit of a playboy, I bet.

Matthew No no. Divorced. My wife and I used to live in this flat, then I moved back in with my parents. So now I –

Sandra Divorced! Aha. So, tell me Matthew, what are your decadent Western intentions towards Tere here?

Matthew Intentions? Nothing. I mean . . . The flat was empty anyway, and Tereza said she could do some talks in the school. You know, about what's happening in Eastern Europe. I teach Modern Studies –

Sandra Intriguing.

Matthew (*to Tereza*) I've got a class on Monday. Could you come along again then? Start the discussion?

Tereza I can't do Mondays. I have a regular talk I give on Mondays, to the Czechoslovakia Solidarity Group. Any other day.

Matthew Oh.

Sandra You'll find that out about Tere, Michael. The Revolution first, last and always.

Matthew Good for her. Used to be the same myself.

Matthew punches the air with his clenched fist.

Tereza (*to Sandra*) Didn't you say you had to go soon? Meet your boyfriend or something?

Sandra *You're* the one with the boyfriend.

Tereza (*annoyed*) Well, if you're going to stay, I think we'd better straighten a few things out.

Sandra begins to leave.

Sandra Perhaps you're right. Thanks, Tere. It's been very interesting, don't you think? (*to Matthew*) Excuse me, Michael.

Matthew Matthew. Please. No need to go on my account. I can come back some other –

Sandra No, Tere's right. I really should make contact with base.

Matthew Base?

Tereza Yes she can be.

Matthew Look, I hope I didn't cause any . . . problems here?

Tereza Of course not.

Matthew Pity about Monday. It's the last time I have these kids before the Christmas break.

Sandra puts on her jacket and shoes.

Sandra It's been a real pleasure meeting you, Martin.

Matthew stands up to shake her hand.

Matthew And you. I hope we meet again.

She bends towards him, kisses him lightly. She picks up the flowers.

Sandra (*sadly*) We will never meet again, Malcolm. Ever.

Matthew (*concerned*) Why not?

Sandra You wouldn't understand.

Sandra heads off towards the door.

Tereza Wait! Sabina could do it. *You* take Matthew's class.

Sandra stops dead.

Matthew That's a good idea. Would you?

Sandra No. Of course not. I mean, that's Tereza's thing. I can't –

Matthew and Tereza stand at either side of her.

Matthew It's no big deal. It won't even be in the classroom. I thought I'd take them out to a café, let them relax. It's not a speech or anything, just a chat.

Tereza Sabina would be perfect. She is the living embodiment of the Czech struggle.

Matthew It would be good if you could do it, Sabina. The kids were really looking forward to meeting a real dissident.

Tereza Then it's perfect. Of course she'll do it. Won't you, Sabina?

Matthew I'll meet you beforehand, if you like. Brief you, as it were.

Tereza What time, Matthew?

Matthew Three o'clock. I'll meet you at two, in the café. I'll give Tereza the address.

Tereza That's settled then. Right, Sabina don't let us keep you back.

Sandra Tereza. Could I have a word with you for a moment?

Tereza Certainly.

Tereza goes over to the door.

Sandra (*whispers*) Are you mad!

Tereza Me! I'm just teaching you a lesson. See where dishonesty leads?

Sandra You going to tell him after I've gone?

Tereza I will not! *You'll* go along on Monday, and *you'll* tell him. He's going to be very disappointed. In more ways than one, I imagine. As far as I'm concerned, you both deserve it.

Sandra This is stupid. I'll tell him right now.

Tereza On you go.

Sandra Matthew.

Matthew Yes?

Pause.

Sandra See you Monday.

She turns to go, whispers to Tereza, stuffing the flowers into her hand.

You've asked for it. You raised – I'll see you.

Tereza What?

Sandra Now you've got a real bet on your hands.

Tereza You'll lose.

Sandra I hope it pisses down on your revolution

Tereza (*out loud*) Thank you so much. See you tonight, Sabina.

She goes. Tereza returns to the centre of the room.

Matthew She's a very nice girl.

Tereza All us Czechs are. That's why you brought *me* the flowers, wasn't it?

Blackout.

SCENE TWO

Late evening. Same room. Dripping of rain. A key in the lock, the door opens. Matthew and Sandra tumble into the room, soaking wet and laughing. Sandra has Matthew's anorak wrapped around her.

Sandra So that's what you call cats and mice.

Sandra kicks her shoes off.

Matthew Dogs.

Sandra Dogs and mice?

Matthew No – cats and dogs. Raining cats and dogs.

Sandra I love it when it rains dogs and cats and mice.

Matthew You wouldn't if you lived here all the time.

She takes off the anorak; throws it on the sofa.

Sandra Why do you people complain about the weather all the time? Rain is so . . . sexy. Don't you think? The drops run down your back, like little fingers, stroking you.

She shakes the rain out of her hair.

Matthew You've got great hair. You just don't get that colour this far west.

Sandra You Scottish boys – you're such gentlemen.

Matthew Where's Tereza?

Sandra Out giving one of her talks, probably.

Matthew steps a little closer to her.

Matthew Bet she's not as good as you. Christ, you made some impression – I've never seen those kids so fired up.

Sandra It's all because of you – you're a good teacher.

Matthew Me? Nah. Hopeless. But the kids today – reminded me of myself, when I was at school. Thought I was a right rebel. I used to walk about with a copy of *Das Kapital* hanging out of my school blazer. Till my mum confiscated it cause it ripped the seams.

Sandra What a rebel.

Matthew Some rebel. The only problem I had was when the heidie once caught me –

Sandra Heidie?

Matthew Sorry. Head Teacher. Suspended me for wearing my school tie round my head. Then I realised it was all pointless.

Sandra It was very brave of you.

Matthew Wrong revolution though, eh? A stupid kids' game. Here's me trying to make everyone more like you, and you're trying to make everyone like us.

Sandra But at least you tried to change things.

Matthew No no no. It's pointless trying to change anything. Things are the way they are. We all have to accept that. Face up to our individual responsibilities.

Sandra But I *want* to change things! I want everything to be new. They say in the papers that there will soon be a 'Third Way' in my country. A third language, even. That sounds nice.

Matthew Third Way my arse. Sorry – that's Scottish for 'unlikely'.

Sandra Your language is so exquisite. It rings in the ear like little bells.

Matthew That what I . . . *really like* . . . about you. You see everything as being so wonderful. You're so . . . generous. Here you are, a refugee, an exile, no work, no money – yet, last night you wanted me to reduce Tereza's rent.

Sandra She has nothing. I have a little money left . . . from Berlin.

Matthew Berlin?

Sandra Just make it less for the whole flat. Tere and I will sort it out between us.

Matthew Problem is – my ex is taking me for everything. That's the difference between you two. You're so kind. She's a bitch of hell.

Sandra In my Third Way, there'd be no money.

Matthew (*laughs*) You're such a dreamer. There is no Third Way.

She leans towards him . . .

Sandra Oh, I don't know. I'm sure I can think of something.

Matthew I bet you can.

The sound of a key in the door. Sandra jumps up.

Sandra Shite!

She smooths down her dress. Tereza enters, in a hurry.

Tereza Quick. Where's the radio?

Sandra Hi! (*exaggerated accent*) Tere! Good of you to come home early to join Matthew, and little Sabina.

Tereza (*searching for radio*) Not clicked yet, Matthew?

Matthew Sorry? We're getting along fine.

Tereza finds the radio, kicks off her shoes, takes off her coat and hat.

What's happened?.

Tereza There's been trouble in Wenceslas Square.

Tereza turns the radio on.

Radio Voice Fifty thousand people thronged into Wenceslas Square chanting 'Freedom – now or never!' Riot police moved in on them, surrounding the square and cutting off the demonstrators' escape. From my position above the square, I could see police clubbing the young people at random. Already reports have come in of one fatality at police hands. Mirolas Stepan, the Prague Party boss, made the following public statement earlier today –

Tereza turns the radio off. She turns, glares at Sandra.

Tereza Who wants to hear any more lies.

Sandra (*quietly*) I give in.

Tereza Oh no, you don't!

Sandra This is crazy. It'll have to stop.

Tereza I'm not convinced yet.

Matthew Not convinced! Listen to what the man said – it's happening! Now.

Sandra I thought you didn't believe in games?

Tereza I do in this one.

Sandra You'll lose.

Tereza We'll see.

Pause. Sandra and Tereza look at one another. Silence.

Matthew What is it with you two! Look, I'm new at this revolution game. (*to Sandra*) But this is no time to start talking of giving in! (*to Tereza*) And this is no game, Tereza. This is the real thing. Come on! There's work we can do here. Sabina – do that thing you did with the kids again.

Sandra Not now, Matthew.

Matthew Give me your lipstick. I'll show her.

Sandra Tereza doesn't want to see that.

Tereza On the contrary – I'd be fascinated.

Tereza Here. Have mine.

She gives him lipstick.

Matthew Right. (*Goes to the window.*) Pretend this is a map of Europe, right? That's Russia up there. Now, if you draw a St Andrew's cross from . . . where?

Sandra Franz Josef Island.

Matthew Franz Josef Island in the north east, here. To the Azores in the south west, here. Then from Greenland –

Sandra Iceland.

Matthew Iceland, in the north west. To Crete in the south east . . . That's the four corners of Europe, right?

Tereza Not necessarily.

Matthew Well they're as good as any other four corners. But using these, where do you think the centre of Europe lies? Eh?

He taps the middle of the window.

Tereza No idea.

Matthew Austria? Geneva, maybe. Bet you think it's Prague.

Tereza Where is it, then?

Matthew Two miles south east of Motherwell! (*to Sandra*) That'd be around Craigneuk. Craigneuk's the very epicentre of Europe! Would you believe it? Craigneuk?

Tereza (*to Sandra*) Very impressive. Where did you find all this out?

Sandra I . . . worked it out one night. In Berlin. When I was waiting for my false passport to come through.

Tereza Of course.

Matthew That kind of stuff really woke 5A up. She makes them feel important, like they matter.

Sandra It only works on a very small map.

Tereza Perhaps we should change your duties from Undercover Operations to Public Relations.

Matthew Undercover Operations – seriously? You never think these kinds of things really happen.

Sandra It sounds better than it really is. It's a bore, really.

Matthew (*to Tereza*) You should, you know. Get her out amongst the public more. She's a terrific act.

Tereza Don't I know it.

Matthew (*to Sandra*) Come and speak to the teachers next.

Sandra I think I've done enough.

Matthew But –

Sandra We'll talk about it over dinner.

Matthew Yeh, sure. (*to Tereza*) I promised this girl a slap-up meal for doing the class.

Tereza What about all the classes I did for you before?

Matthew Oh yeh. Of course. Well, then. Join us, if you like.

Tereza No no. I don't want to spoil things. Oh. I've just remembered. Sorry. I'm afraid I must disappoint you.

Don't you remember, Sabina? This is the night Prague contacts us for our instructions?

Sandra Is it?

Matthew D'you want me to stay? See if there's anything Prague would like me to do?

Tereza It's getting far too dangerous now, Matthew. The less you know, the better for you.

Sandra (*to Tereza*) Can I walk him to the bus stop?

Tereza So long you don't get on the bus with him. (*to Matthew*) You know what us Czech women are like on buses.

Matthew I haven't a clue what you two are talking about half the time.

Matthew hands Sandra his coat. She puts on her shoes. They exit. Tereza gets up, listens.

Tereza Still not fixed that fucking leak!

She finds the radio, turns it on, carries it into her bedroom.

Radio Voice Further reports are coming in of the fatality during the demonstration in Wenceslas Square. A young student has not been seen since he was made to run a police gauntlet. Police deny that Martin Smid has been killed.

Blackout.

SCENE THREE

Matthew, shirt-tailed and bare-footed, sits on the couch; Sandra, bare-legged, lies with her head on his lap.

Sandra The Rivers' Kiss. That's what maminka used to call our house.

Matthew Your whatka?

Sandra Maminka. Mum. Because it's just like a little castle, nestling between the Berounka and the Elbe. In the woods. Not far from Prague.

Matthew Sounds nice.

Sandra At night it's so dark there you can't see anything at all. It's like you could have died. But the trees reach out and stroke your skin to let you know you're still alive.

Matthew strokes her legs.

Yes, like that. There's a little stream that runs off the river and flows right through the cherry trees behind the house. Before they sent me away, I used to go out to it, early in the morning, and lie in the water.

Matthew Wasn't it cold?

Sandra Freezing. It made you scream out. But the feeling of the water sparkling on your skin and running through your hair and down your legs . . .

Matthew runs his fingers down her legs.

Matthew Like this?

Sandra Like that.

She shivers and gives a yelp.

Matthew Ssshh! Tereza.

They listen for a sound from Tereza's room. Nothing. They laugh quietly.

What about your family? Your mother and father. Did they prance naked through the trees with you?

Sandra My old man? Stalwart of the Politburo? Dancing naked?

Matthew Your father's in the Politburo?

Sandra The Butcher of Bohemia, they called him –

Matthew And you a dissident! I take it he didn't know?

Sandra He'd have had me strung up.

Matthew Did your mother know?

Sandra Maminka died before all that began. She would have understood, though. My sister knew. Sondra.

Matthew She's still over there?

Sandra Last I heard she was in hiding.

Matthew So how did *you* get out of the country?

Sandra They raided our newspaper office and arrested most of our comrades, but Tomás and I managed to escape.

Matthew Tomás?

Sandra An old friend.

Matthew You mean boyfriend.

Sandra Comrade-in-arms. Anyway, we lived out in the woods for a few weeks until the fuss died down.

Matthew Was he into skinny-dipping too?

Sandra Well, under the circumstances our clothes didn't last long.

Matthew I bet they didn't.

Sandra Do I detect a note of envy?

Matthew The entire Prague Symphony. Go on.

Sandra It was a long time ago, in another lifetime. Anyway, we made it to East Germany.

Matthew How?

Sandra I had to pose as a prostitute to get a truck driver take me through the border. I distracted him, while Tomás hid in the back of the truck.

Matthew How did you do that? Distract the driver.

Sandra In the usual way.

Matthew Oh.

Sandra Then we made our way to Berlin. East Berlin, so we were still in hiding, of course, and couldn't stay in the same place for very long – Tomás and I wandered around the city for days and days. Alone, lost in this big, strange city . . .

Matthew No doubt good old Tomás kept you warm.

Sandra Tomás said we were like a lost brother and sister.

Matthew Heard it.

Sandra He said we weren't really making love to each other but to ourselves.

Matthew Nice one.

Sandra He said we were simply making love to the people we'd like to be.

Matthew Guy's an expert. I suppose you'll go back to him . . . once this is all over?

Sandra No. (*sighs*) We lived for the moment back then. You had to. To survive. Tomás and I have had all our moments. Now, it's moments with you.

Matthew Christ – I can't compete with Humphry Bogart there.

Sandra Of course you can.

Matthew gets up.

Matthew Kidding? This guy's risked his life. All I ever risked was my school blazer.

Sandra You still have the rebel in you. I can sense it.

Matthew It's easy for the Tomáses of this world. You try to find an evil despot to slay in Maryhill.

Sandra And I thought they were everywhere.

Matthew You find me one, and I'll batter him for you. Nah. It's a drag, just facing up to reality every day.

Sandra (*sadly*) Funny, and I remember you so defiant at school. You had so much hope.

Matthew Yeh. Prat . . . You *remember*?

Sandra Oh, I'm sorry. My English. I mean I remember you saying.

Matthew Well, not any more. I'm cured of dreaming. Thank God. Look what it did to Czechoslovakia.

He comes over to her; puts his arm round her.

You make me feel like fighting. Anything. Anyone. I'll risk my life, if you want, for your 'Third Way'.

Sandra That's what Tomás used to say.

Matthew Christ, this guy Tomás never shuts up, does he? That was my best line – and he said it first.

Sandra *You* are my Tomás now. Together we'll change the world. And now that I've got a real person to make love with, there's no need to do it alone.

They kiss.

Matthew I don't think I can stand this kind of talk another second. Come on. I'm all of a tremble.

Tereza appears at the door of her room in her dressing gown.

Tereza You're Oliver who? Did he just say he was Oliver Cromwell?

Sandra I don't think so.

Tereza Thank God for that. Another code name would finish me.

Sandra Sorry. Did our talking wake you?

Tereza sits down

Tereza Not the talking. Earlier. I thought Russian tanks had rolled into your room. Not that I mind. But singing the opening lines of the Czech National anthem at the height of your ecstasy was a bit much to take.

Matthew Is that what it was?

Tereza God, I found myself joining in with you.

Tereza sits down on a chair.

Actually, I came out to give you the news from Czechoslovakia.

Sandra Did you now? Funny how revolutions keep happening at awkward moments.

Tereza I know. It's so boring, isn't it? Just when you're doing your best to secure East-West relations.

Sandra So – what has happened?

Tereza A big demonstration through the city centre. Everybody chanting 'To the Castle', and jingling their keys. You could hear them on the radio. It sounded like a million tiny bells ringing.

Matthew Why do they do that?

Sandra Czech fairy stories always end with a bell ringing and the storyteller saying 'and that's the end of the story'.

Tereza (*to Matthew*) They're telling the régime the game's up.

Matthew And *is* the game up?

Tereza gets up.

Tereza You tell me, Matthew. Is it?

Matthew Looks like it to me.

Tereza A disappointment, I imagine, for you?

Matthew Disappointment! I'm on your side!

Tereza But, when it's all over. Sabina will have to leave.

Matthew I know.

Tereza Better act quick. You don't want to lose your little dream girl, now do you?

Matthew But by then Czechoslovakia'll be a free country.

Tereza And if we lose?

Tereza exits.

Matthew She's right. I don't want to lose you.

Sandra Matthew. There's so much you have to learn about where I come from.

Matthew I know, I know. Your real life. This is just a holiday, isn't it?

Sandra I'm beginning to wish it weren't.

Matthew You'll go back to Tomás.

Sandra I told you – you are my Tomás now.

Matthew It's okay. (*Takes her hand.*) Sabina. I understand more than you think. You've been denied freedom all your life, it's understandable than when you get it, you go to town on it. I'm just glad that you chose me to play with. You can tell me as much or as little as you like. Trust me.

Sandra puts his arms around her.

Sandra Maybe. Maybe you will be able to understand. We'll see. But not now.

Matthew No. Not now. We've other things to do.

They kiss.

Hang on. I'll just get a map of Czechoslovakia. You can tell me the whole story again.

Matthew goes into another room. Tereza enters from her room.

Tereza Well, I admit. He's more of a lack-wit than I thought.

Sandra He's not a 'lack-wit'. I'm just very, very good at being Sabina. It's easier being Sabina than Sandra. Now *that's* a difficult role to play. Nothing to get your teeth into. So – have I won? Can I let him go?

Tereza Do you want to let him go?

Sandra I don't know.

Tereza Well, as far as I'm concerned, this matter is not over between us.

Sandra Come on!

Tereza For all you know he might be playing you along. To get what he really wants.

Sandra I don't think so.

Tereza You haven't really tested him yet.

Sandra How do I test him?

Tereza Get him to propose. In front of me.

Sandra For God's sake!

Tereza I need to know that people prefer the truth. You admit defeat if you want to.

Matthew (*off*) I'll bring the map of Scotland, too. See if I can find something sexy about Stirling!

Sandra I can't now. Not just like that.

Tereza For his sake or yours? Either way suits me. You both need taught a lesson.

Sandra Couldn't Sabina be called back to Prague? Leave the poor guy with his memories?

Tereza No! There are rules. Either admit defeat and tell him. Or get him to propose. Those are my terms.

Sandra I'll tell him tomorrow.

Matthew enters, with a pile of books.

Tereza Oh no, she's not sent you for books! You don't *have* to read them, you know. Take up smoking, apparently it's more acceptable

She heads back to her room.

Matthew You know – you can be pretty weird at times.

Tereza Me? We'll see who's weird.

She exits; he goes to Sandra. Blackout.

SCENE FOUR

Sandra sitting alone in the room. She is playing with the now-withered flowers, pulling off the dead petals. Speaks in her own accent.

Sandra He loves me, he loves me not. He loves me, he loves me not. He loves Sandra, he loves Sabina. Sandra, Sabina; Sandra, Sabina. He's a prat. No he's not.

(*She gets up; wanders the room; picks up a book. Reads, in Sabina accent*) 'I am merely defending my own identity in conditions I did not invent.' (*Sandra accent*) That's easy for you to say, Vaclav.

(*She slumps down onto the sofa.*) Sandra Hamilton. Everyone's always told you – you're a waster. A sleekit wee keech.

Jangling of keys in lock. Matthew lets himself in. Sandra jumps up.

To je ostuda! Matthew. You gave me a fright.

Matthew That Czech you were talking? Funny, some words sound dead like Scottish words. I was passing by. Thought I'd drop in.

Sandra Shouldn't you be at school?

Matthew I'm taking the rest of the morning off.

He throws her the keys.

I shouldn't really be letting myself in, should I? Here.

Looks in his inside jacket pocket. Takes out money.

And while I'm at it. Here.

Sandra What's this?

Matthew I was thinking. You're right. Two penniless dissidents. I shouldn't be charging you. That's the first month's back again. If you can handle the electricity and everything.

Sandra But I thought you were skint. I mean impoverished. Take it back – you need it for the alimony.

Matthew That's another thing. Saw my ex this morning.

Sandra Oh.

Matthew She's still a pain, but we made our peace. Promised I'd sell this place. Once you two have gone, of course.

Sandra splits the money in two.

Sandra We'll give this to Tereza. I don't want mine.

Matthew Don't be daft. You're skint. Oh – that must've been where you got that word from, eh? Me.

Sandra (*thrusts the money into his hand*) Please. I don't want it.

Matthew You revolutionaries. So independent. (*Takes money*) Okay, I'll hang on to it for now. I'll put it away, you're bound to need it later. Christ – I'm going to end up paying you to leave me!

Sandra We'll put this here for Tereza. You're in a generous mood today.

Matthew That's down to you, babe. I feel like a new man. Only one thing wrong, but.

Sandra What's that?

Matthew Well, I'm hardly acting like your perfect capitalist ally, am I? You're trying to kick the Commies out, and here's me – half Karl Marx, half Cilla Black.

She goes to him; takes off his jacket, slowly.

Sandra Half Sean Connery, my big Scottish man and a half.

Matthew James Bond, actually. Oh no. I forgot. You're the spy.

Sandra And I'm going to investigate every inch of you.

She pulls him to the couch; kissing his neck.

Matthew I'll come quietly.

Sandra Oh, don't do that.

Matthew Better enjoy it while I can. Might not last long.

Sandra I'm sure you can make it last very long.

Matthew I mean, apart from you having to go back one day, the way I'm acting, we're going to be on opposite sides.

Sandra That sounds interesting.

Matthew Seriously. I'm coming over all idealistic again these days – just as you've had enough.

She stops and looks at him.

One day, we might be looking at each other down the barrel of a gun.

Sandra It's possible.

Matthew We'll work something out. Now what about this interrogation? You going to blindfold me?

Sandra Good idea. We'll do that later. I've got another idea. A game Tomás and I used to play.

Matthew Not Tomás! I don't want to hear about him right now.

Sandra No – you must understand. Tomás is just a word I use. It means lover.

Matthew It means some great Slavic guy keeping his bed warm for you in Prague or Berlin or wherever.

Sandra No. I made the name up.

Matthew You mean there was no one in Berlin?

Sandra No. Yes. But his name wasn't Tomás. I call all my men Tomás.

Matthew Christ. There must be a Euroglut of Tomáses!

Sandra Now you are my Tomás.

Matthew (*to himself*) Oh well, live for the moment, Tam. What was it this other Tomás used to do?

Sandra Search strip. Is that what you call it?

Matthew Strip search. But I like it both ways. (*Nazi accent.*) Right. Step this way, Slavonic slave. Take off ze clothes!

Sandra No. *I'm* going to strip search *you*.

Matthew Wey-hey! Strip away, Mrs. Stalin.

She comes over to him, then changes her mind.

What?

Sandra You do it. Strip for me. Now. Now! Strip!

Matthew begins to take off his clothes. After his shirt and socks, he pauses at his trousers.

Matthew I've got nothing on me, Madame. I swear.

Sandra I think I can see something illegal. Continue. Strip!

Matthew is unsure how to progress. He decides to do a strip-tease act for her.

Matthew Yes! Yes! Anything you say. I am totally in your power! I'll do it – only, please, please don't hurt me.

Trousers off, he stands still, embarrassed.

Now what?

Sandra Let me see. Remember the stream I told you of? In my garden, in my little village in Bohemia?

Matthew I'm not really dressed for travel.

She lies out on the couch

Sandra I want you to be my stream. Run over me, like the sparkling water. Make your body into waves. Flow over me.

Matthew Can I do that? Yeh. I can do that.

He comes over to her, begins to wriggle down her.

Sandra Yes, like that. It's as if I were home at last.

Matthew I am the Great River Tomás!

Sandra You see the magic of Tomás? With a new name, you can be whoever you like. Who would you like to be?

Matthew thinks for a moment; then quietly:

Matthew I want to be your lover. Your secret lover. You can hide me away in your tiny village. All day I'll wait for you, planning the revolution. And we'll make love until we're old and grey. And then we'll still make love. And be loved by everyone, for vanquishing poverty and oppression and boredom, the world over!

Sandra I like that.

Matthew Then let's tell the world! Now!

Sandra (*alarmed*) No. It's our private world!

He rushes to the window. Opens it, stands in front of it and shouts out:

Matthew I am Tomás! I am Sabina's slave! (*He pulls back from the window.*) Oh shit. Mrs McNulty.

Sandra Who?

Matthew Head of Guidance. Oh, what the hell.

He waves out the window. Then shouts, louder:

I love Sabina Vasiliev!

She comes up to the window. He turns to her.

Sandra Do you?

Matthew Yes.

Neither notice Tereza enter quietly. Matthew shouts out the window again.

I love Sabina! I will do anything my Slavonic Princess says!

Tereza Will you now?

Matthew Hello. Excuse me.

He grabs all his clothes. Exits, running, to dress. Once he exits:

Tereza My heavens. You're nastier than I realised. You'd have been a star in the régime back home.

Sandra It wasn't like that.

Tereza No?

Sandra No. We were enjoying ourselves. I wasn't trying to make him do that.

Tereza What's this guy *like*?

Sandra Good. He's a good man.

Tereza He's a dunder-pate.

Sandra A what?

Tereza A dizzard, a donkey. Dolt. A hoddy-doddy.

Sandra Is that English or Czech? (*angers*) Leave him alone! Anyone would look stupid, if you catch them in their private moments.

Tereza Then you shouldn't have private moments in the front room of *my* flat!

Sandra *He* owns it. And I live here, too!

Tereza I take it you've got your proposal?

Sandra No. Please. Enough's enough. Let Sabina disappear. I've taken it too far, now.

Tereza I consider myself a woman of honour. I'll make you a deal. If you do get him to propose – in front of me – your reward will be to let him go, without knowing who you really are.

Sandra And if you win – what do you get?

Tereza Peace of mind. The knowledge that people always prefer the truth. That they will fight against lies and deception.

Sandra Just let go of it, will you?

Tereza Letting go is up to you, Sandra. You can call it off at any time.

Pause.

I didn't think so. You're a coward. The truth is everything.

Sandra But I'm not lying! I'm more me when I'm Sabina than when I'm Sandra. Sabina fits me like a glove. I feel like me when I'm her.

Tereza What kind of honesty is that? It is all right that he thinks you are Sabina? You are *not* Sabina! You should tell him you are Sandra. For once do the decent thing and tell the truth. I still have enough faith in human nature to believe that he won't do it. In his heart, he knows this is all a . . . sham. Take it to that point. We'll see.

Matthew enters, dressed, reading a paper, trying to act nonchalant.

Matthew Says here Jakes won't make it to the new year. (*reads*) 'Vaclav Havel confidently predicts a Free Czechoslovakia by Christmas.' That'd be nice, wouldn't it?

He sits, burying himself in the paper. Tereza sits beside him.

Tereza Except that Sabina won't be here for much longer.

Matthew I know.

Tereza So you have to make plans. Prepare.

Matthew Make plans?

Tereza You've waited long enough. You've been patient. But the time must come to make a move. Sabina knows that, don't you Sabina? You are a good rebel. You have been making plans. Go on, tell him.

Sandra Tereza.

Matthew Tell me what?

Tereza Ah, you know how Sabina can be so shy about these things. This is your moment, Sabina. Act. Now.

Matthew What is it? You can tell me.

Sandra (*goes to him*) Nothing . . . It's just . . . that –

Tereza Sabina! She gets so tongue-twisted about these things. What she's trying to say, Matthew is . . . (*to Sandra*) Which is it to be, Sabina?

Sandra looks lost

Sandra Not now, Tereza. This isn't the moment.

Tereza Oh, but the vital moment to strike has arrived, Sabina, surely. The waiting game is over. Take heart, Sabina. Be resolute. Tell him. Now. Which it is to be? Decide!

Sandra I can't!

Tereza (*angrily*) Right. Then I'll decide for you! Sabina wants you to do the decent thing – go back with her to her little village in Bohemia. Isn't that right, Sabina? And you – you'd love to go, wouldn't you, Matthew?

Matthew Yes, I would.

Sandra No!

Tereza Oh, it would be a such shame for him not to meet your family.

Matthew I'd like that.

Sandra We'll talk about it later.

The two women look at one another for a moment. Sandra defiant

(*Brightly*) Right! Fine. Okay. I'd love you to come, Matthew. Next spring, maybe. For a holiday.

Tereza Oh no. That's far too long to wait. If the predictions are right, Matthew, you could spend Christmas in Prague. Our city is beautiful at that time of year, isn't it Sandra?

Matthew That would be fantastic.

Sandra I doubt if that'd be possible. Next year, maybe, when –

Tereza I tell you what. Make it official. Why don't the pair of you get engaged!

Matthew Well, I'd just been thinking that –

Tereza There you go, Sabina! A winter wedding in Free Prague!

Sandra Wedding! That's going too far.

Tereza Oh Sabina, could I be bridesmaid? Please? We could have a garden party at the Castle.

Sandra Don't rush him! (*to Matthew*) We'll talk about it later. When we're alone.

Matthew Okay. If you want.

Tereza But you will consider it?

Matthew If I thought for a moment that she'd have me . . .

Tereza And you have no doubts?

Matthew On my side, no, but –

Tereza And you are absolutely convinced about Sabina here?

Matthew Yes, but –

Tereza (*angry*) Right. That settles it! It's over!

Pause.

Matthew What's over?

Pause.

Tereza You have proved yourself to me, Matthew. I had my doubts. But now I am certain that you and Sabina are perfect for each other!

Matthew Oh, you needn't have worried. I love her.

Sandra Matthew, there are things I have to tell you first.

Tereza Plenty of time for that. At the party.

Sandra What party?

Tereza Oh, we need to have a party. To celebrate this great occasion.

Matthew Don't know if there is an occasion yet. (*to Sandra*) That's up to you. But I'm all for celebrating. What time?

Tereza Nine o'clock? Not here. In the bar.

Matthew I'd better get back to school. (*to Sandra*) There's something very important I have to do there. A decision I've come to.

Sandra What?

Matthew I'll tell you about it tonight. Then I'll go home and get my glad-rags on.

He kisses Sandra on the cheek. Exits.

Tereza And I must get ready, too. (*to Sandra*) And you must get dressed up. You like getting dressed up.

Sandra I haven't got anything to dress up in.

Tereza I'll find something for you. After all, this is Sabina Vasiliev's One Big Night. You might as well get it right.

Tereza exits. Sandra sits on the couch. Pause.

Sandra Jesus.

Pause. In the silence, we hear the radio being turned on in Tereza's room.

Radio The Czech Police have failed to produce Martin Smid – the student who went missing after the demonstration in Wenceslas Square. It is now believed that he has died in police custody. The Martin Smid incident continues to fuel the rebellion against the Government.

Silence again, as radio is turned off. After a moment Sandra jumps up.

Sandra Aw, fuck it! Go for it, Sabina!

Exits to her room. Blackout.

SCENE FIVE

The seats have been re-arranged to resemble a bar. Tereza and Matthew, waiting for Sandra.

Matthew What's keeping her?

Tereza Changing.

Matthew Eh?

Pause.

Tereza She takes ages to change.

Matthew Never noticed.

Pause.

So what's keeping her?

Pause.

Tereza Perhaps she's been detained.

Matthew Detained? By who?

Tereza By *whom*. Just detained. Late. Relax, please. You have a big night ahead of you. Conserve your energies.

They wait a moment longer, until Sandra arrives, in a long coat. Matthew goes to her. Tereza and Sandra nod to each other apprehensively. Sandra sits between them.

Pause. Then she turns to Matthew.

Sandra So what's this decision of yours?

Matthew I've quit my job.

Sandra What!

Tereza You fool.

Matthew I didn't do it for you. I did it for me. It was killing me, that job. I need a change, that's all. New horizons. I feel great about it.

Tereza Like a lamb to the slaughter.

Matthew So, come on. Let's get on with the party.

Sandra It may be our last party, Matthew. I might have to go away.

Matthew What! Where?

Sandra We were contacted by Prague this evening. They might want me back there. (*hesitantly*) That's right, isn't it, Tereza?

Tereza They suspect her of being a double-agent.

Matthew Oh, get lost!

Sandra Either I go back, or . . .

Matthew Or?

Sandra (*brightly*) I will have to take up a new identity here! Pretend that I am not Czech all together. Give myself a Scottish name, invent a past – a very ordinary, boring past – for myself.

Tereza Oh no you don't!

Matthew With that accent? And the way you look? You'd never pull it off. Christ, Tereza here would have a better chance!

Tereza She must face charges.

Matthew (*to Tereza*) I don't believe you. 'She must face charges'! What is it with you tonight? It was your idea we had a party.

Tereza Some party. I'm fed up with liars and idiots.

Sandra Tere! We had a deal!

Matthew What deal?

Sandra I can't divulge the content of the information from Prague. This might be our last night together, Matthew . . . for quite a while. Please, let's just enjoy ourselves, this one last night.

Matthew There's something you're not telling me. Was that why you were late ? Did Tomás get in touch with you?

Sandra and Tereza look at one another.

Tereza Tomás? Who is Tomás?

Matthew Her lover. In Prague.

Tereza (*angry, to Sandra*) You even stole him from me?

Matthew Christ. Did you get off with her boy-friend?

Tereza What did she tell you about him?

Sandra Don't, Matthew. Keep it our secret.

Matthew (*to Tereza*) He escaped the country with her. He's still hanging out in Berlin.

Tereza In Berlin! Tomás is in a prison at home. Half-starved, locked up for three years now!

Sandra (*Scottish accent*) You never told me that.

Tereza Why should I? I have my own private world, too. It had nothing to do with you!

Tereza separates herself from the others.

Sandra (*Czech accent*) I told you, Matthew. Tomás is just a name I give. You are my Tomás.

Tereza You couldn't lick his boots.

Matthew I'm getting pretty confused here. Anything else I should know?

Sandra Please, let's not ruin this night.

A stand off between them. Tereza breaks it, by jumping up brightly.

Tereza She's right! I'm sorry. We're supposed to be celebrating Sandra's victory!

Matthew What victory? Who's Sandra?

Tereza Sabina – you must sing for us. That's what we always do in our country, isn't it? The lady who we are celebrating always performs one of our beautiful Czech songs for everyone. I'll go and speak to the musicians.

Sandra Tere!

Matthew Oh go on, Sabsy.

Tereza Sabsy! Dear God!

Sandra No – I can't!

Tereza Don't believe a thing she says, Matthew. Sabina is wonderful performer. Go on, Sabina. Reveal yourself.

Tereza strides up to the musicians.

Matthew What's going on?

Sandra She's upset.

Matthew Why?

Sandra Lonely. Worried about her people at home. And we had a bit of a falling out.

Matthew About what?

Tereza returns.

Tereza They're waiting for you.

Sandra gets up. Matthew bewildered. Tereza smiling broadly. Sandra speaks to her quietly.

Sandra Please. Don't ruin everything. Not now.

Tereza Oh, I'm sure you'll find a way out of it. You always do. Go! Enjoy! You've won!

Sandra is about to go, but lingers, holding Matthew's hand.

Sandra Matthew. I do love you. That's the truth.

Then she goes. The others sit and watch as the musicians begin to play. Sandra steps slowly, hesitantly on to the stage.

(*Announces*) Unfortunately, the musicians don't know any of our Czech songs. So I will sing a song in French instead.

Then, she takes of her coat; is spectacularly dressed underneath. She sings with relish:

Déshabillez-moi
Déshabillez-moi
Oui, mais pas tout de suite
Pas trop vite
Sachez me convoiter . . . hmm

Me desirer . . . hmm
Me captiver!

Matthew She speaks French as well?

Tereza Of course. Studied it at your University here. Until she got bored.

Matthew Here?

They turn their attention to Sandra.

Sandra (*sings*)
Undress me
Undress me
But not all at once
Not too fast
Learn to want me
Desire me
Captivate me!

Matthew Sandra?

Tereza Sandra Hamilton. From Maryhill.

Matthew And Sabina?

Tereza Me, more or less. She stole my life. My lover. But won a bet.

Again, they turn to watch Sandra.

Sandra (*sings*)
Déshabillez-moi
Déshabillez-moi
Conduisez-vous en homme
Soyez l'HOMME!!

    Agissez!

Déshabillez-moi
Et vous . . .
Déshabillez-vous!

The music ends.

Matthew What bet?

Tereza That you wouldn't fall for it.

Matthew gets up to go. Tereza holds him back.

Tereza Come round tomorrow. You'll see.

Matthew leaves. Sandra watches him go. Looks at Tereza.

Sandra You promised. You lied.

Tereza See what lies can do?

Sandra sits, looking towards the door. Tereza slowly gets up to leave. Exits. Sandra sits for a while alone; then gets up and follows her

SCENE SIX

Tereza standing on a chair, changing the light bulb in the desk lamp. It flashes on as she does so.

Tereza Cert to vezmi! You hoor you.

Matthew enters.

Matthew Charming.

Tereza You know who you can thank for that.

Matthew comes in to centre stage; looks around.

Tereza Shoes.

Matthew What? Fucksake.

He kicks off his shoes.

Where is she?

Tereza In her room

Matthew Then get her out here.

Tereza What are you going to do?

Matthew What d'you think? Give her a bollocking.

Tereza A what?

Matthew Give her a piece of my mind. Let her know what she's done to me.

Tereza And me.

Matthew You?

Tereza I agree that we should show her we are angry, but shouldn't we be a little bit more subtle?

Matthew Fuck subtle! I can't be arsed with subtle!

Tereza So I see. This 'bollosking' you talk of – will it do any good?

Matthew It'll do me good.

Tereza But will it change Sandra's behaviour? Punishment should correct the behaviour that caused it. Will this bollosking method you speak of achieve that?

Tereza wanders round the room, thinking.

Matthew I don't know. But it'll make me feel better.

Tereza Perhaps we shouldn't be too harsh on her. I'm not suggesting that her crimes go unpunished, but eventually, we must accept her apology.

Matthew You can accept an apology if you like. Not me. I don't care how sorry she is – I'm not accepting any apology.

Tereza comes up to him.

Tereza You are a decent man, Matthew. If my heart can soften, so can yours. But I agree that it is healthy to show anger. At least at first.

Matthew goes towards room

Matthew Too true. I'm going to haul her out of there.

Tereza holds him back; she goes towards the room.

Tereza Let *me* bring out our little Rusalka. And remember – you and I must stand firm, no matter how much she excuses herself, or cries. We must do our duty.

Lights dim. Before Tereza reaches the door, it opens. Sandra steps out. She is wearing a blindfold.

Matthew Christ!

Tereza What on earth are you doing?

Sandra talks faintly, in her own accent.

Sandra Lead me to the chair.

Matthew Take that thing off!

Sandra finds her way to the table, sits.

Sandra Begin.

Tereza Begin what?

Sandra The interrogation.

Matthew Aw, in the name of God!

Tereza Enough of these games!

Sandra gropes around looking for the lamp.

Sandra This is no game. This is what you want, isn't it? Have your revenge. Where do we begin?

She finds the lamp, turns it towards herself and switches it on.

Matthew Why shine the light in your eyes if you're blindfolded? Not think you're maybe overdoing things a bit?

Tereza Are you trying to make a fool of me now? And my people. What we have to go through?

Sandra I have no intention of making a fool of anyone. Do you want my name or not?

Matthew Jesus. She's a complete bam.

Silence for a moment.

Tereza Very well then. Play your little game. It suits our purposes perfectly, Matthew. Name?

Sandra hesitates a moment.

Sandra Sabina. Sabina Vasiliev.

She speaks in Sabina accent.

Matthew Och, in the name of God!

Tereza It's not even a Czech name!

Sandra For the purposes of this interview, my name is Sabina Vasiliev.

Matthew Chuck it with the phoney accent, will you? Gets on my tits.

Sandra It used to get you on mine.

Matthew Shut it!

Sandra I will answer your questions as Sabina Vasiliev. This situation is not pleasant. Sandra Hamilton could not withstand it – so you will have to deal with Sabina. I repeat, I am Sabina Vasiliev. Czech, by formation. And inclination.

Matthew You're seriously damaged goods, that's what you are.

Tereza Very well. You are charged with being an imposter. How do you plead?

Sandra Sandra Hamilton pleads guilty on any charge you wish. She has asked me to apologise deeply, but she wishes to add that I – Sabina Vasiliev – was at no time involved in these crimes.

Matthew Oh no, you're not wriggling out of it that easily!

Tereza (*to Matthew*) We have to find a way of making her realise the gravity of her actions.

She gets up; goes to Sandra, unties the blindfold. Sandra blinks, looks at Matthew. He turns away from her. Tereza picks up the gun, points it at Sandra.

Matthew Jesus! You're not going to shoot her?

Tereza How far would you like to take the game of playing revolutionaries, Sandra? My father used this gun to fight against the Fascists. He gave it to me as a reminder that we must always fight against those who would rob us of our dignity.

She lays it down.

Now I'm reminding you.

Pause.

Why did you wish to make a fool of Matthew, me and my people?

Matthew Yeh – why me? Why pick on me? Did I just walk through the door at the wrong time?

Tereza No, no Matthew. You were chosen. You were the prefect guinea-pig.

Sandra You would never have been interested in Sandra Hamilton.

Matthew For all you know, I might have liked Sandra. I mean you.

Tereza Ah, but you see, that's what made you so perfect, Matthew – you *knew* Sandra Hamilton.

Matthew No I didn't.

Tereza Oh but you did – you were at school with her. Wasn't he, Sabina?

Sandra nods. Pause.

Sandra You lit her bunsen burner once.

Matthew I what! Jesus.

Sandra She was the little mousy girl, the year below you.

He stares at her.

Matthew I don't remember.

Sandra I know.

Sandra gets up; walks around.

Sandra I didn't think that you'd . . . (*Sandra accent*) . . . fall for me.

Matthew Oh, and I fell for you all right, didn't I? Hook, line and sinker. Undercover operations. Maminka. The Butcher of Bohemia?

Tereza You're as bad as she is.

Matthew Everyone told me she was Sabina! You – you did! She spoke the language, as far as I knew. She knew everything about bloody Czechoslovakia. And I wasn't the only one who fell for it, by the way! The kids at school, the teachers. There was even that woman once –

remember? She knew you. Called you Sandra. You even managed to convince her you weren't you. Even . . . even, the River's Kiss? That too?

Sandra hangs her head. Matthew sits down in Sandra's seat – the light shines in his eyes.

Tereza And you? Are you so dismissive of my people and our struggle, that you could fall for her pathetic act for so long?

Sandra He simply believed what he saw.

Tereza Perhaps that's your problem, Matthew. You want to believe too much.

Matthew Who wouldn't? Oh look – let's just forget all this.

Tereza Too late, Matthew. The stone's begun to roll. Let's see where it stops.

Matthew Maybe I kind of knew all along. I, just, didn't want to see it. Is that so bad? Things were going well . . . I felt, stronger. (*to Sandra*) I gave up a lot for you. For Sabina. I thought you were the real thing. Now I look at you, it's obvious you're just an ordinary wee punter.

Sandra Matthew. Look at me. I'm the same girl I was yesterday. The same colour of hair. Same eyes. You fell in love with me. I'm the woman who loved you.

Matthew Love! How can you use that word! All that . . . crap, you gave me. Samizdat press . . .

Tereza That was me.

Matthew Having to prostitute yourself to escape.

Tereza That was *not* me! Oh you must have loved that, Matthew. Your own private little whore. (*to Sandra*) So, what – all us Czech women are prostitutes, now?

Sandra I read it somewhere. That's how some women escaped.

Tereza By putting their lives in danger! Not to turn their boy-friends on! How dare you! You stole my struggle, my life, even my Tomas. Ah but, you were right, Sandra. *Two* foreign women – he would have fallen for both of us.

Matthew I never fell for you! And I didn't fall for *her*, because *she* doesn't exist. Hang on a minute. How come I'm the one on trial here? I'm the victim, remember?

Matthew turns the light on Tereza.

What about your responsibility in all of this?

Tereza *Mine?*

Matthew Yes – yours. Playing along with her. Having a good laugh at my expense.

Tereza It was *me* who told you the truth! I admit – I made a tactical error. I thought you would have . . . come to your senses . . . sooner than you did.

Matthew You mean you thought I couldn't be as stupid as all that. Well, there you go: I am.

Tereza Sandra was more accomplished than I suspected.

Matthew (*to Sandra*) Did you have all this planned before you even moved in? (*to Tereza*) You helped it along. You collaborated. It was *you* who suggested that she speak to my pupils in the first place. You set the whole thing up.

Tereza You disgusted me. Both of you. All of you. Your boredom bored me. Everyone I've known till I came here was fighting for their freedom. Of course, you don't need to. You've got your freedom. And what do you do with it?

Matthew Perhaps it's *you*, Tereza, who wants to believe too much. D'you want to know what'll be the first thing over the border of Free Prague, Tereza? Eh? Pornography, drugs. You wait and see.

Tereza I thought you'd have been happy about that! Isn't that what Sandra here supplied you with? I don't need cheap political lessons from someone who's never fought for anything in his life. Freedom is indivisible. You're either free or you're not.

Sandra steps out of the shadow.

Sandra Precisely.

Pause.

I admit it. I wanted to be like you. Sandra Hamilton was never given the chance. But Sabina – she had a history. Fire. Passion. She fought back. Sabina changed things. Changed the kids at your school, you said so yourself. Changed herself. Even changed you, Matthew.

She goes to Matthew.

She wants to leave a message for you, before she goes. A message for her Tomás. She says, if you're ever passing the Rivers' Kiss – and you will one day – Sabina'll be waiting for you.

She kisses him lightly on the cheek.

Pause. Then Matthew grabs her.

Matthew There is no Rivers' Kiss. No Sabina. Just Sandra Hamilton.

He goes to Tereza.

You see what she's done? She's turned us two against each other.

Tereza moves away from him. Then stops, thinks. Turns. Slowly, she goes back and stands close to him

Tereza Perhaps you're right. She's had her fun with us . . . Let me ask you something . . . you say you fell in love with Sabina?

Matthew (*to Sandra*) How can you fall in love with someone who doesn't exist?

Tereza Perhaps she *does* exist. What was it you fell in love with? Her romantic past, yes? The fact that she was a dissident? A freedom fighter?

He shrugs.

Her home in Czechoslovakia.

He nods.

How she dressed. The way she spoke.

Matthew Yes, yes.

Sandra Please, Tere. Don't.

Tereza ignores her.

Tereza The idea of a new life in another country, with an exotic woman? You fell for a . . . an amalgam. Like the police make up. An assembly of eyes, clothes . . .

Matthew A photo-fit.

Tereza A blow-up doll, like they sell in magazines –

Matthew No! I thought it was more than that.

Tereza Perhaps it was. That woman does exist.

Pause.

Sandra Stop it.

Tereza It's very hard, you know. Watching a man – like you – fall in love with someone who's pretending to be me. It should have been me! Tell me, do you still want to go to Prague?

The game dawns on Matthew. He turns to Tereza, gets closer to her, but looks at Sandra

Matthew Nothing else to do now.

Tereza Then come with me. I know I'm not nearly so exotic as Sabina. Perhaps I could get my hair dyed to look more Slavonic.

Matthew Your hair looks beautiful.

Sandra Matthew. Stop it!

Tereza And my body isn't so bad, is it? Matthew, isn't it about time you found out if you could love a *real* woman? Not a fantasy.

She touches his arm. Her accent becomes more pronounced.

Matthew I thought I did love a real woman.

Tereza You know I've always . . . liked you, don't you? What do you say again, I have . . . what is it? *Hots* for you? I want you. Fancify you. Unless of course, it's too late for us.

Sandra For God's sake. Now she's playing Sabina.

Matthew stares over at Sandra, then back at Tereza; takes her assertively by the arm.

Matthew It's never too late. We still have time, before your revolution. Let's go, before you fade like a dream, too.

He leads her towards her bedroom.

Sandra Matthew!

They keep walking. At the door, Tereza stops and looks round at Sandra.

Tereza exits to bedroom; Matthew remains at the door.

It's the game, isn't it? You're still playing the game?

Matthew Am I?

Sandra Of course you are.

Matthew That's the problem with this game of ours, Sabina, isn't it? You never know where you stand.

He turns to go.

Sandra Matthew. For God's sake.

He exits. Sandra stands, cries.

Radio A student who had been thought dead, killed in the demonstration in Wencelas Square, has turned out to be alive and well. The authorities admitted last night, that he had not been killed. The emergence of a non-existent martyr who has fuelled so much of the Czech rebellion, is an exquisite irony for a nation that has had its fair share of real martyrs.

Sandra exits to her room. Blackout.

SCENE SEVEN

Dead of night. Sandra wanders round the room.

Sandra Ceskoslovensko. Skotsko.

Pause.

At home, when I was young I used to play by the stream in the garden of the Rivers' Kiss. When it got dark, Maminka used to tell me stories. We sat by the water, and her voice washed over me like a wave. She told me the story of Snowflake.

Once upon a time it was wintery winter, all over the world. And in this winter there was a little girl – just like you, Sabina. The little girl had no-one to play with, so she made herself a friend – a snowgirl. She made her out of the cold, lifeless snow. She gave her long, white, snowy hair, and an icy sparkling dress. And she named her new friend Snowflake.

But then, when she made delicate lips of ice on her snowfriend, the little girl stood back, startled. Did she feel warm breath on her hand? Then Snowflake moved. She shook the loose snow from herself, and held out her hand. She was so pretty, and kind and gentle, that the little girl soon lost her fear.

All winter long, the little girl played with her new friend, whose eyes were as blue as the sky, and her words rang out bright and clear like crystals.

And around the little girl's cottage, so sad and silent for many years, there now echoed the happy chimes of the two friends' laughter . . .

And then the thaw came.

She looks at the gun in her hand. Brings it up to her face. Opens her mouth, points the gun inside. After a moment, she pulls the trigger. Blackout.

Pause.

Lights go up. Sandra gets up, returns the gun to the bookshelf.

Sandra And that was the end of the story.

Lights cross-fade to next scene. Tereza enters . . .

SCENE EIGHT

The sound of bells ringing – joyfully, like Christmas. Tereza is packing some of her things in boxes, listening to the radio.

Radio Last night, Vaclav Havel, the leader of the dissident movement, declared 'I am among you again', and announced the success of the Czech Revolution. It now looks likely that Havel will become the first writer of fiction to become President of his country. The crowds cheered, and rattled their keys, and church bells chimed, when the new leader told them: 'It's time for champagne'.

The doorbell rings.

Tereza It's open.

Matthew enters sheepishly, his hands behind his back.

I've been expecting you.

Matthew How've you been doing?

Tereza Okay.

He nods towards the radio.

Matthew Great news. Heard it last night. Thought maybe I should come round and wish you congratulations.

Tereza stops packing; smiles.

Tereza Thank you.

Matthew reveals from behind his back a bottle of champagne, flowers, and three glasses.

Matthew Like your man said: time for champagne.

Tereza pauses for a moment. Then smiles, comes over to him.

Tereza Why not?

Matthew The war is over, eh?

Tereza *Three* glasses?

Matthew Yeh. Is she in?

Tereza Probably. Hardly ever see her these days.

Matthew Does she still think . . . you and I . . .

Tereza shrugs.

Matthew When are you leaving?

Tereza Today.

Matthew Can't wait to get back to the old country, I bet?

Tereza You bet.

Matthew Look. About . . . all this. What happened. I'm –

Tereza Like you said – the war's over.

Matthew I'll just go and see if Sandra's there.

Tereza I've tried to speak to her, but she just mopes around all day. Think I preferred Sabina.

Matthew goes towards Sandra's door. As he goes . . .

Matthew Listen.

Tereza What?

Matthew Nothing. Silence. So you got the leak fixed?

Tereza Yeh. A few days ago. I presumed you'd organised it.

Sandra – dressed as Sabina – enters. But she speaks in her Sandra accent.

Sandra No. It was me. I went to the council on Friday morning. They sent someone round straight away. (*Sabina accent*) 'I am so sorry to trouble you. Your great country has made me a guest, when my own poor country is in a shameful mess. And here I am complaining. Please forgive. But you are such wonderful, wonderful, warm-hearted people here, and everyone talks to you at bus-stops. And so humorous – so funny. I love you. But my doctor has told me that one more drip and I may die. (*feigns tears*) Dubcek flu. A killer for Czechs in capitalist countries.'

Tereza And she fell for it?

Sandra Nah. She just wanted shot of me. (*to Matthew, sheepishly*) Hello.

Sandra goes to Tereza .

Congratulations.

Tereza Thank you.

Matthew Champagne, then?

Sandra Bubbly? Yeh!

Matthew pours out three glasses; they take one each.

Nazdraví!

Tereza Nazdraví!

Matthew Bottoms up.

They chink glasses; drink.

Sandra goes to the drawer, takes out the money. Hands it to Tereza.

Sandra Matthew decided weeks ago, you shouldn't be paying rent. So I've been saving it for you. You'll need it now.

Tereza hesitates for a moment. Then takes it. Sandra turns to Matthew.

It's all there. I'm not a thief.

Matthew I didn't say a word!

Tereza Thank you Matthew. And you.

Tereza finishes her glass.

Right. I'm going to get the rest of my things together.

She exits to her room. Matthew and Sandra awkward for a moment.

Sandra Aren't you going to go with her?

Matthew What would I do in Prague?

Sandra Find yourself a Sabina. Place must be hoaching with them.

Matthew One was quite enough for me.

Tereza enters, with her coat and hat and a bag.

Sandra Is that you?

Tereza That's me.

Sandra What about your books?

Tereza I can't carry them. You have them. You had more uses for them than I did.

She goes to Matthew, then turns to Sandra.

How does it go again? (*Turns back to Matthew. Exaggerated accent*) 'Your beautiful country has made me a guest. Please forgive.'

Sandra Keep working on it. You could pass for Czech yet.

Tereza goes to the door. She looks around.

Tereza I hope you two come to . . . a compromise. (*to Sandra*) Goodbye, my little Rusalka.

She exits, slowly. Sandra watching her, tearfully.

Sandra Farewell Czechoslovakia.

Matthew What an impression we must have given her.

Sandra Ach, you know what foreigners are like. Get all emotional about the slightest little thing.

Matthew What will *you* do now?

Sandra Thought I might reapply to Uni. Boring, eh? Maybe try doing Czech and Russian.

Matthew Think I should try my hand at one of them? I've always been crap at languages, but –

Sandra First time for everything.

Matthew Maybe . . . you could teach me – the basics?

Sandra Yeh. Sure. Thought I might give classes anyway. The grants these days.

Matthew Yeh.

Sandra I was going to put a sign up in the corner shop. What d'you think? Czech tuition; apply within. Sandra Vasiliev.

Matthew Sounds good . . . *Vasiliev?*

Sandra (*Sabina accent*) More chance of getting pupils if they think you're a native speaker.

Matthew But you're not!

Sandra To je ostuda! As a matter of fact, Vasiliev's my grandmother's name.

Matthew Oh no – don't, Sandra. Don't start.

Sandra Cross my bra and hope to die.

Matthew Heart, not bra. Christ, what am I saying! You know that!

Sandra She was a White Russian.

Matthew A White Russian in Maryhill?

Sandra Lady Olga. Handmaiden to the Tsarina Catherine. The Reds thought they had killed her, but she escaped. It's true!

Matthew For crying out loud – you expect me to believe . . .

Sandra begins to exit, then turns, adamant.

Sandra When all's said and done, Matthew – what choice have you got?

She puts on her coat. Speaks again in Sabina accent.

If you want to come, we shall discuss these classes.

Matthew No

Sandra Well. Bye, then. Remember, my River Tomás. Sabina is waiting for you at the Rivers' Kiss.

They look at one another for a moment. She blows him a kiss, and with a flourish, exits. The sound of bells ringing, growing louder.

Matthew Bye. White Russian. What does she think she is? A fucking cocktail?

He paces around.

Sandra Vasiliev? *Sandra* Vasiliev. What does she take me for? A madman? And what if I am? Ach, to hell with it!

He goes to the door, the bells getting louder.

Sandra! Wait! I'm coming! Wait for Tom! Sabsy!!!!

The bells reach a crescendo, then stop. Blackout.

Ends.

The Nonduality Diary

Mike Jenkins

Copyright © 2013 Mike Jenkins

All rights reserved.

ISBN: 10:
1481889435
ISBN-13:
978-1481889438